For Naomi and all her dreams.

—L. S. G.

For Seth, always.

—S. F. C.

Blue Ridge Babies 1, 2, 3

Laura Sperry Gardner

illustrated by **Stephanie Fizer Coleman**

A COUNTING BOOK!

PAGE STREET KIDS

Over in the Blue Ridge in the leaf-dappled sun
lived a gentle mother deer and her little fawn **ONE**.
"Hide," said the mother. **"I hide,"** said the **ONE**.
So they hid in the forest full of leaf-dappled sun.

Over in the Blue Ridge where the skies are so blue
lived a mighty mother bear and her little cubs **TWO**.
"Forage," said the mother. **"We forage,"** said the **TWO**.
So they foraged ripe berries where the skies are so blue.

Over in the Blue Ridge in a budding dogwood tree
lived a regal mother cardinal and her little fledglings **THREE**.
"Fly," said the mother. **"We fly,"** said the **THREE**.
So they flew through the air round the budding dogwood tree.

1

Over in the Blue Ridge where the white oak branches soar
lived a wise mother owl and her little owlets FOUR.
"**Hoot**," said the mother. "**We hoot**," said the FOUR.
So they hooted bright and clear where the white oak branches soar.

Over in the Blue Ridge off a steep and winding drive
lived a busy mother groundhog and her little chucklings **FIVE**.

"**Dig,**" said the mother. "**We dig,**" said the FIVE.
So they dug and they burrowed off the steep and winding drive.

Over in the Blue Ridge in a thicket full of sticks

lived a clever mother fox and her little pups SIX.

"Pounce," said the mother. **"We pounce,"** said the SIX.
So they pounced and they darted through the thicket full of sticks.

Over in the Blue Ridge where the mountains fade to heaven
lived a keen mother rabbit and her little kits SEVEN.
"Nibble," said the mother. **"We nibble,"** said the SEVEN.
So they nibbled dandelions where the mountains fade to heaven.

Over in the Blue Ridge mid the poplars tall and straight
lived a playful mother squirrel and her little squirrels **EIGHT**.

"**Skitter**," said the mother. "**We skitter**," said the EIGHT.
So they skittered and they scurried mid the poplars tall and straight.

Over in the Blue Ridge where the crooked creeks combine
lived a swift mother brook trout and her little fry **NINE**.
"Swim," said the mother. **"We swim,"** said the **NINE**.
So they swam and they splashed where the crooked creeks combine.

6

5

8

4

7

9

Over in the Blue Ridge in a boggy mountain fen
lived a mother salamander and her little efts **TEN**.

"**Slither,**" said the mother. "**We slither,**" said the **TEN**.
So they slithered in the mud of the boggy mountain fen.

Over in the Blue Ridge where the forest children play,
every creature has its place, every family has its way.
"**Grow,**" say the mothers. "**We grow,**" say the young.
So they're growing in the Blue Ridge in the shadows, streams, and sun.

WHAT IS THE BLUE RIDGE?

The Blue Ridge Mountains are part of the Appalachian Mountain Range. These ancient mountains are covered in thick forests that create a misty haze. From a distance, this mist makes the mountains appear blue, which is how they got their name.

Barred Owl
Mother owls lay two to five eggs, one at a time, as many as four days apart. The first owlets may be up to two weeks older than the last.

White-Tailed Deer
When they are young, fawns have white spots that fade when they are older. The spots help them blend in with patches of sunlight that shine through the forest leaves.

Groundhog
Groundhog mothers will whistle to alert their babies to danger, which is why some people call groundhogs "whistle pigs."

Eastern Gray Squirrel
Squirrels are very talkative and make lots of different sounds. Mother squirrels use special sounds just for babies. Many describe these sounds as "coo-purring."

Red Fox
Red fox pups have gray fur when they're born, but it changes to red in the first month.

American Black Bear
Bear cubs are born during hibernation and stay with their mothers until they're about a year and a half old.

Eastern Brook Trout
Mother trout lie on their sides and beat their tails up and down to clear a spot where they lay their eggs, then cover them up and leave them to hatch.

Eastern Cottontail Rabbit
Mother rabbits will have several litters per year, with four to twelve kits in each litter.

Northern Cardinal
Baby cardinals start out with gray bodies and no feathers. As they grow up, they develop a crest and feathers. Males become bright red and females become tawny brown.

Northern Red Salamander
Baby salamanders start out as efts that live in water and breathe with gills. Later, they grow legs and move onto land, where they breathe using lungs.

This counting rhyme is based on a poem by Olive A. Wadsworth and is set to a traditional tune. Sing along with the Blue Ridge edition!

OVER IN THE BLUE RIDGE

Lyrics by Laura Sperry Gardner

Traditional

O - ver in the Blue Ridge in the leaf dap-pled sun lived a gen - tle mo-ther deer and her

lit - tle fawn one. "Hide," said the mo - ther. "I hide," said the one. So they

hid in the for - est full of leaf dap - pled sun.